AF715708

How to Become the Millionaire Next Door 4th Ed.

Kay Duncan

Published by Kay Duncan, 2011.

While every precaution has been taken in the preparation of this book, the publisher assumes no responsibility for errors or omissions, or for damages resulting from the use of the information contained herein.

HOW TO BECOME THE MILLIONAIRE NEXT DOOR 4TH ED.

First edition. June 19, 2011.

Copyright © 2011 Kay Duncan.

ISBN: 979-8231955954

Written by Kay Duncan.

*"To the unsung millionaires—the teachers, engineers, small-business owners, and hardworking individuals who build wealth not through luck or extravagance, but through patience, wisdom, and relentless consistency.

This book is dedicated to those who live below their means, invest diligently, and prioritize financial freedom over fleeting status. To the parents who teach their children the value of a dollar, the dreamers who reject debt, and the disciplined souls who understand that true wealth is measured in security, not symbols.

May your journey be steady, your habits unshakable, and your legacy enduring."

—Kay Duncan*

Wealth is what you choose, how you focus and design your life.

How to Become the Millionaire Next Door

Kay Duncan

Chapter 1
Ego

Ego is the single worst enemy of any person who wants to become a millionaire.

You can become financially successful when you understand the methods of attaining and more importantly keeping wealth.

More than seven million United States households presently have a net worth of over one million dollars excluding the primary residence. Most of that wealth has been created within the last decade due in part to a strong economy.

Investment researchers predict the millionaire march will continue by fifteen percent annually.

You will be glad to hear that it is not rocket science. It is actually easier to become the millionaire next door than you could ever begin to imagine.

The secrets are simple.

You do not have to make certain that every person who meets you on the street knows that you are making money. You need not be arrogant or pretentious to make money. You do not have to drive the most expensive vehicle, wear ridiculously expensive designer clothing, or in any way flash your wealth.

It will be due in part to this lack of arrogance and pretentiousness that you will be able to become the millionaire next door. It is also why you will remain solvent while some of your friends will sadly go broke.

Ego is the single worst enemy of any person who wants to become a millionaire. You ask, "Why?"

Because arrogance is only preceded by ignorance.

This one principle can cause you to be your own worst enemy and prevent you from attaining the goal of becoming a millionaire.

You cannot allow your ego to be too big for your own financial good by spending what you cannot afford to pay for with cash.

You do not have to brag that you make a killer living, spend money like it grows in the backyard garden and flaunt that you do not want to be seen at the flea market. If you are guilty of any of these or pretending that you are a big money maker, then you are letting your ego speak loudly for you. Your ego is leading you around by the nose directly to being stone cold broke.

It is not necessary to give the impression that you are dripping in money. Most people are smart enough to figure out if you are trying to keep up with the Jones.

Here is a surprise for you—the Jones you think are millionaires are probably not millionaires.

It is a mistake to attempt to keep up with the Jones and support an expensive lifestyle you cannot afford.

Do not attempt to support a lavish lifestyle.

You do not have to eat at the most expensive restaurant in an exclusive area of town or buy at high price clothing boutiques.

It is not necessary if these things are far out of your reach. This is especially true if you are putting your purchases on credit when you have little if no money in savings.

Without having money in savings, you will not be able to produce that incredible idea you come up with that could become a potential big-time moneymaker or go into business for yourself.

Producing a product from concept to finished marketable product requires money.

Nine hundred dollars in savings is hardly enough to invest in marketing a new product.

You will have to save your money.

Do not let your ego talk convincing your friends that you have a huge bulk of money in savings when in reality you are not a saver, but rather a spender who many times spends more than you can afford. You cannot bury your responsibility and continue to spend way beyond your expendable income level.

The sole purpose of ego spending is to impress others. It is putting on the dog and the truth is you will not impress anyone.

Do not allow your ego to become your single worst enemy without realizing it.

People who have real hard money do not feel the need to impress. They know they have money. They do not let their egos drive them to arrogantly display their wealth. That is a sign of insecurity.

Do not look up to anyone who spends money unwisely.

There is the false notion that others look up to people who presumably have money. Do not let this drive you. It is okay to have the desire to have other people look up to you.

Used incorrectly it can take you directly into the poorhouse when you should be the millionaire next door in the prime of your life.

Chapter 2

Purchase well. Sell smart.

You will need to learn how to purchase well and sell smart. Learn to be a wise spender and budget your money.

Look up to those people who are wise spenders and try to learn from them. They can teach you.

This wise-spender mentality has nothing to do with the amount of money a person has in the bank, but rather everything to do with not spending yourself broke. You can have millions pass through your fingertips and spend yourself into the poorhouse by being irrational with the way you spend your money.

Just because you have money in the bank does not mean you have to spend down to the last dime. You have to learn there is a line to be drawn in the amount of money you will allow yourself to spend.

You know it as budgeting.

Any time you buy something you need to make certain that you are getting the absolute best buy for your money. This means you must research the price. Your goal is to attempt to purchase with the idea that if you had to sell the item you could at least get out of it what you paid for it or, even better, you would be able to make a profit on it should you decide to sell it.

If you decide to buy a pair of wave runners, be aware that brand new a single wave runner may start at approximately ten to fifteen thousand dollars. A new pair means you will be looking at approximately twenty to twenty-five thousand dollars not including the dual trailer, life jackets, saddle bags, and other paraphernalia to go along with the purchase. You will be looking at a total purchase of around twenty-five to thirty thousand dollars.

When you hear monetary figures let your ears perk up. You should be thinking that is a lot of money to spend for equipment for entertainment purposes, especially for something that will be rarely used. If so, you are thinking exactly along the lines that the millionaire next door thinks.

Those with egos will be thinking that they are too good for anything but the absolutely most expensive brand-new wave runners. It is all about the fact that others will see them and they have to make it look like they can afford the best. More power to them as we watch them finance their prize possessions only to watch those possessions lose huge value the minute they are driven or pulled off the lot.

Are you laughing now? If not, you should be. If it sounds like yourself, hopefully you are on a quest to change and become the millionaire next door.

If you have the money to pay cash for a new pair of wave runners, you should only be looking at new wave runners, trailer, and gear to price shop. You should not even take it under consideration to purchase new. Your goal is to settle on a pair of used wave runners evenly matched with trailer and gear for a price that when you decide to sell you get exactly what you paid if not more.

This is smart purchasing.

The goal is to try to purchase the item after the initial drop in price like the loss that a new vehicle takes the minute it is driven off the lot.

There is nothing wrong with purchasing used.

Millionaires purchase used yachts, used wave runners, used sailboats, etc. The list is endless. They sell those same items for more than the purchase price two and three years later.

When you purchase something, purchase it with the thought in mind that you may have to or you may decide to sell it and if you do, you will need to at least get your money out of it and hopefully get more than you paid for it.

That is precisely the nature of the deal and exactly what will make your money expand into millions rather than diminish.

If a piano dealer offers you $1,200.00 for an antique player piano that you paid $100.00 for, consider selling it unless you sincerely wish to learn to play the piano on it.

Anything you own should be for sale at the right price.

As long as you are being offered enough money that you are willing to part with your belongings, sell, sell, sell.

Chapter 3

Focus

Your focus is wrong if you are comparing your financial status and buying what others have.

Stop drooling over what everyone else has, comparing your financial status to those you know and purchasing just so you can have what someone else owns.

This can be detrimental in your quest to becoming a millionaire. Your focus is wrong. There is nothing wrong with wanting what everyone else has. It is okay to want it, just not to the point that you place yourself in financial jeopardy by buying what you cannot afford.

If the truth were known about everyone else's finances around you (you know the ones you think are wealthy) you would soon discover the majority of them are living on borrowed money. Their beautiful extravagant homes are mortgaged, their brand new expensive cars are leased, and their credit cards are used extensively which means they are paying unnecessary high interest. They are not as rich as they appear. Their bottom line is bright red. That is the fact behind the financial facade that most of these people display. Do not get caught up in those trappings or you will never become a millionaire.

Instead you must buy what you can afford, meaning what you can pay cash for. You must buy when you can afford it meaning again,—when you can pay cash for it.

It is not that difficult to do. It does not matter how bad you want a new car or a bigger home. If you want to become a millionaire you have to get with the millionaire program.

You must do without the things you want and purchase the things you need.

You "want" a candy bar. You do not "need" a candy bar. This is such a perfect example in a small way that can be compared to the large things you think you need when in reality it is the things you want, not need.

There is a major dollar difference between the things you want and the things you need. This difference can be the fine line between whether or not you become a millionaire.

Consider doing without a second vehicle even if you have the money to buy a vehicle. You may be able to pay cash for a vehicle. With the amount of money you have in the bank, consider carefully whether or not you can be comfortable spending it on a vehicle. You may find that after second thought you are more comfortable leaving your money in the bank.

Let the "what ifs" cruise through your head of how easily you could be in financial trouble if you part with your cash to buy a vehicle.

It may not be the easiest route for you. It may mean your spouse will have to wait to go the store. It may mean that your friends might think you are unable to afford a second vehicle. Do not let it matter in the least what others think. You will know the truth about your financial status. That is all that is important in accomplishing your goal to be a millionaire.

When you must make a need purchase make it an informed purchase.

If you have to purchase boots for your child's school trip to a cold climate, shop until you know you are getting the best buy for your money. Compare sales flyers and ask the manager to match another store's lower price for the same or like pair of boots. Do not let it matter to you whether or not the manager thinks you are or will become a millionaire, just get the best buy for your money on every penny you spend.

Chapter 4
Be yourself

Never let what other people might think deter you from becoming a millionaire.

This is a classic mistake many people make. It is easy to become ensnared in trying to keep up a financial appearance for everyone else around you. Do not do it.

Do not buy anything to show off. That means nothing, whether it is designer clothing, a brand-new car or an apartment or house that is not well below your financial ability whatever it may be. You know what it is that tempts you.

We all have those temptations to buy something outrageous. Let it pass and pass on purchasing it. Leave your money in the bank or leave it invested in those items you can return your money on. Spend your money on the important things you need and spend it for you not for anyone else with the exception of spending it on your family's needs.

Do not rent an outrageous New York high rise apartment that you cannot afford to impress a slew of young women or men you bring over to your pad. Keep the reality behind your façade to appear wealthy in check. You do not need to pinch literal pennies to pay to live in a breathtaking apartment, have no food in your refrigerator and have to go home to your mother's house in the country to wash your clothes and eat.

Move into a place you can afford, buy a washer and dryer, and stock your refrigerator. Do not consistently present yourself as having a lot of money. The result is you will keep yourself broke. You will also attract the wrong kind of attention from shallow men or women gold-digging for someone with money. The minute they discover the truth they will be out of there and you will be bringing in a new treasure-chasing gal or guy. This scenario will repeat itself constantly until you break the cycle.

Do not put on the dog and present yourself for who and what you actually are and have to offer. You can be wonderful with much to offer without being pretentious. The right man or woman will fall in love with you for all your qualities not your implied money or lack thereof.

Chapter 5
Pretentiousness

Do not be financially pretentious.

This can be a double-edged sword and prevent you from achieving the goal of becoming a millionaire in many ways.

To the listener who gives the financial braggart an ear: be wary. Usually the financial braggarts are the ones with little to no money and nothing but a big mouth.

If you own a full line manufacturing and you greet any salesman who walks in off the street, it is not necessary that you feel the need to tell everyone that you met in the plant or does business with you that you own the business. You do not need to feel that sort of insecurity about yourself. It can work to your advantage if salespeople merely think you are nobody.

Salespeople will say what is on their mind and, more often than not, drop their guard around employees revealing what kind of person they are behind their sales pitch simply by opening their mouth. It is funny what salespeople will tell the employee, but not the owner. You will be able to weed out the ones who are not giving your company the best deals and are trying to push products on your company that you do not need to purchase.

By never being financially pretentious you will get the best deals on products. You can save hundreds of thousands of dollars on items that you purchase for your company if you purchase manufacturing items for the best possible price. You must cross check every item that comes in to the plant to make sure you are paying the price you are quoted and it is not being billed at a higher price. You must also check to be certain that you cannot get it cheaper anywhere else.

Replace a part you are paying $1.10 for .08 times 30,000 parts and you can save your company $30,600.00 on one order. That is $30,600.00 in profit and no telling how much profit in the long run.

Never let it be beneath you to say you cannot afford the price that you are being quoted or tell the salesperson you can get it cheaper elsewhere. Constantly ask your suppliers to match a different company's prices.

You do not have to be loyal to any one company. Buy from the person that gives you the best price and delivers on the date that you need the product.

As long as you are not financially pretentious you will always get the best deals. You will pay less and get more for your money.

No matter how much money you make you will always need to attempt to pay less for items and get more for your money in the bargaining.

No matter how rich you are, how much money you have in the bank, how much you think you can afford to pay more for items, it all adds up in the long run and diminishes your final net worth if you pay too much. Those small increments off your bottom line add up to one big red minus entry. It also significantly reduces the quality of your standard of living.

Your wedding company is asked to host a wedding on a 1.5 million-dollar 104' yacht. You realize a wedding would mean a tremendous amount of guests on a beautiful yacht in the wrong footwear for the boat. High heels can virtually ruin the deck. You are in need of three hundred pairs of boat shoes for the guests to wear on your boat.

You do not go to Dillards to buy three hundred pairs of boat shoes. You go to Kmart.

Smart millionaires and those who want to become millionaires are not too good to buy at Kmart, Wal-Mart, and other bargain stores.

You enter a wonderful high-end linen store for the first time. You love the store. The buyers are obviously very good, but the items for sale are expensive. You spend a good hour in the store wandering around looking at the store's merchandise and checking prices. You find a small

30" fiber optic Christmas tree that you want for $40.00. You should consider whether or not that is too much to spend on it and maybe pass on the purchase. Two days later, you might find the exact same tree at a different store for $10.00.

If you would have spent the $40.00 without blinking an eye, you need to stop for a moment to consider what you could do with the $30.00 difference. If you were to shop until you found the same tree for $10.00 you would have $30.00 left over to spend on something else more important like food. You could also do without the tree altogether and save the entire $40.00 for something you need rather than something you want.

If you are thinking that reconsidering a forty-dollar purchase is petty, then you are missing the point altogether.

Chapter 6

Pettiness

In order to become and stay a millionaire you have to become petty on the smallest of purchases.

You are shopping for cans of free stone peaches for a peach pie. You initially purchase them for $1.99 a can at Albertsons. Then you continue to check the price of peaches at Publix and Winn Dixie as you shop at each store getting the sale items and best bargains per store. Winn Dixie has them for $1.19 a can. It takes four cans to make one peach pie. You buy four cans at Winn Dixie for a total price of $4.76 and return the four cans you bought at Albertsons for $7.96. With the $3.20 difference you buy Italian sausage for spaghetti sauce. You could make it simpler, keep the cans from Albertsons, and not bother to return for the $3.20. If you had done that, you would not have had the money to purchase the sausage and you would have been minus that particular meal.

Chapter 7
Snobbery

Do not let snobbery bull dose you into spending more than you feel comfortable spending.

Your child brings home a sheet of paper to the parents of the fourth graders asking for "donations" of services or products for a party for the fourth graders. You phone one of the ladies in charge and ask her about the list of goods. It includes invitations, food, drinks, paper goods, decorations, etc. You mention paper goods. You have paper cups in increments of fifty. You ask if perhaps you could send your child with fifty white paper cups.

She states, "We have 217 students. No, we would want them all to match."

"Thank you," you state, "You've told me all I needed to know."

The difference between this lady and you is you would have graciously accepted fifty white paper cups. The sheet of paper asked for a donation. That means she takes what you are willing to offer, not that she tell you to donate the entire amount of 217 cups that in her words "match".

Snobbery is rampant in the more affluent areas. Do not ever allow someone to make you feel uncomfortable about what you have to offer.

Not everyone was born with a silver spoon. You do not have to donate more than you are willing to part with. Someone else with less self-esteem than you would attempt to save face and offer to purchase 217 matching cups. Do not be bulldozed into giving anything you do not feel comfortable giving. Do not ever allow someone to make you feel uncomfortable about what you have to offer.

This example is self-esteem related. The lady who wants the 217 matching cups hopes you will feel the need to prove something. You do not. She hopes you are not as assured of yourself. All you need to know is that you can afford to buy the best matching paper cups there are, but you are not going to do it, because you see it as a waste of money.

Billionaire Ross Perot would ask, "Hey, what is wrong with plain white paper cups?"

You do not buy a sewing machine when all you need is a needle and thread.

You cannot buy self-esteem. It does not come in dollar amounts no matter how much you spend. You can spend every dime you have and you still will not feel better about yourself.

Work on your self-esteem issues in ways that do not include spending money.

Chapter 8
Clothing

Do not buy yourself poor into designer clothing.

Clothing is such a bad investment. It gets stained and worn out, it goes in and out of fashion faster than you can keep up and you cannot get your money back out of the clothes you have purchased.

Designer clothing is an even worst investment. You might as well have a sailboat with a hole in it, because all you are doing is throwing your money away inside a money pit.

Do not fall for the idea that all millionaires wear designer clothing.

Many millionaires do not wear designer clothing. You can wear whatever you are comfortable in, that might mean a pair of who-cares-what-brand-as-long-as-they-fit blue jeans, plain white tennis shoes, and a non-logo tee shirt.

You want to know who is wearing designer clothes. The ones who want you to think they are rich. This is the manner in which they try to convince you they have money.

Designer clothing is a status symbol that is past the point of ridiculous.

Do not be a designer clotheshorse. Do not spend fifteen thousand dollars on designer clothing in New York City just because you happen to be in the big city.

It is okay to wear designer clothing, but do not be ridiculous with your purchases. Try buying the designer clothing you do wear second hand.

Most people do not care whether or not you are wearing a designer label.

Not everything is money related. Clothing should be comfortable and need only cover your body. It does not have to be expensive.

The richer you get the harder it becomes to find a person who truly loves you for yourself and not for your money. You have to be completely wary of the money-grubbers that it becomes almost impossible to trust someone with your heart. It is not necessary to advertise by the clothing you are wearing that you have money especially if you are advertising because you want companionship. You may find your are advertising for the wrong type of person.

Chapter 9
Confidence

You have to have enough confidence in yourself to know when to stuff your money back in your pocket.

The cashier rings up a price on an item higher than what you thought the item cost. If the price is more than you should pay for that item, pass on purchasing it.

Many people would be embarrassed to pass on a purchase in front of other people, even complete strangers. They might mull in their minds what the people behind them standing in line might think if they do not pay for the item.

You cannot care about what the people standing in line behind you think.

You have to have enough confidence in yourself to know when to stuff your money back in your pocket.

Chapter 10

Entrepreneur

Most millionaires are entrepreneurs.

It is not what you do. It is how much you make and how well you spend your money that makes the difference in whether or not you will become a millionaire.

Millionaires have been known to make their money as garbage men, car salesmen, electricians, you name it. Even bag ladies have been discovered after their demise to have millions in cash stashed away.

You can amass wealth no matter what you do for a living.

It is entirely possible for a carpenter to die leaving over $1,000,000.00 in the bank after giving his children their inheritance before his death.

You can make money in the electrical business, the donut business, the real estate business, the banking business, etc. You do not necessarily have to make your money in any one particular place, but it is necessary for you to position yourself financially to become solvent.

You must be smart with how you spend your money and you must save, so that you will be solvent when financial opportunities knock on your door. You need to be certain you can weather any financial set back, such as, the freeloading brother-in-law file bankruptcy on your company for hundreds of thousands of dollars for goods you have manufactured and then left you unpaid.

Do not be a lender or an enabler to those who ask for money. It is a good policy never to lend family and friends money.

It is a policy that will save you a tremendous amount of grief.

Do not enable those who are careless with the way they spend money, freeloaders who refuse to keep a job and be responsible to themselves, gamblers, non-functioning alcoholics, etc., to mooch off of you financially. It is real simple, when they ask the answer is a resounding, "No."

You are not a bank. If you lend, you might as well give the money away to the person that asked, because you will not see that money again.

If you are going to work for someone else, be a conscientious hard worker.

Many millionaires are entrepreneurs, but there are those that work for someone else all their lives who manage to spend wisely and save throughout their lifetime only to wake up one day and discover they are millionaires. It is perfectly okay if this is the route that you choose. You can still become the millionaire next door.

Not everyone is cut out to be an entrepreneur. It takes a tremendous amount of dedication and discipline. Most people do not have the traits required to be entrepreneurs.

Do not think just because you have shown up for work, you have done the boss a favor.

The only thing the boss cares about is how much money his company makes. He is the one taking the financial risks to give you a job, he is the one entitled to all of the profits and he owes you absolutely nothing that you have not earned. You are dedicating yourself to being his workhorse. So be a workhorse and do it with a smile.

Here is the most important thing you need to remember: if you are not actually bringing in money to the business, you are a deficit. You cost the company money and you are not viewed as an asset except for the work you produce—Therefore, get your butt busy.

The only way you are going to be worth more than the average worker in any business that you do not own is if you are bringing in a cash flow to the company. Think about it.

If you are being paid $15.00 an hour and billing out your time at $105.00 an hour, you are making the company a profit. If you sell $2,000,000.00 worth of equipment and you are paid $50,000.00 a year, the company is making a profit off of your labor. You are a worthwhile asset and may even be worth getting paid more for your labor.

Chapter 11

Opportunity and tenacity

Use your opportunities and never give up.

If you live in a small town where work is scarce, then do whatever it takes to make more money. If you have no children and can work two jobs, then work two jobs.

Take the opportunities that are there and put the extra money in the bank even if it means working a less prestigious job evenings and/or weekends.

You must be willing to lose your ego and use the opportunities that are given to you.

Tenacity can mean everything.

Tenacity is a trait you will have to acquire if you do not have it already in your makeup if you want to become the millionaire next door.

Without tenacity you have given up on becoming the millionaire next door before you have even begun because the minute you bump up against a problem if you are not tenacious you will quit.

Do not quit.

Be tenacious.

Chapter 12

Spouse

Choosing a spouse poorly may be the single worst decision you will make in your entire financial future.

Choose your spouse wisely.

It is important that you choose a spouse that has the same thrifty spending mentality that you do.

If you are thrifty and you choose a spouse that is not thrifty, you have chosen poorly. You cannot baby sit an out-of-control spouse's spending habits.

This may be the single worst decision you will make in your entire financial future.

You should never be involved with anyone who is not 100% up front with their finances. You will never be able to trust them with your financial future.

You do not want to find thousands of dollars worth of bonds hidden in your spouse's briefcase when your spouse had you thinking you were broke.

When someone takes you for a ride financially it is devastating. Building a mass of wealth will take some people their entire lifetime. To be involved with someone who is unwilling to share it with you or to have it taken away from you by a dishonest or selfish spouse is worst than the worst.

Chapter 13
Transportation

Drive your car for transportation purposes only, not to get noticed.

A car is strictly for transportation, although many people think vehicles are a manner in which they show their wealth or lack of wealth.

The most important thing you need is transportation even if it desperately needs a paint job and when you put on the brakes water sloshes in the doors.

It is best if you can pay cash for your vehicle.

You do not have to drive a brand-new car and make payments. Pay cash for a car you can afford and put your money in your bank account instead of in the hands of your banker.

Chapter 14
Budget

You must learn to budget.

Without setting yourself a limit of what you can spend, you will whittle away the money you do make in tiny bits and pieces.

A budget will force you to save for the more expensive things you want. It will cause you to think twice about buying an expensive item. Basically, it will force you to leave the money you make in your bank account.

You cannot spend every dime you make and become a millionaire.

You can throw more out the back door than you can bring in the front door.

People with a knick-knack fetish are a good example of this kind of irresponsible spending.

Do not spend your money collecting designer cows and the like that you pick up in small gift shops. This is a terribly expensive habit with nothing to show for the money spent. Knick-knacks such as this are not worth anything. Do not waste your money on such frivolous items.

If you are going to decorate with anything, do it sparingly. Decorate with taste and remember less is best.

You deserve nice things.

When money is tight you do not spend it on junk. Wait and save your money until you can buy what you want. Do not waste your money on something you are settling on because it is cheap. It is not worth it.

If you will wait and save until you can buy what you really want, you will have nice things—things of value.

That is the kind of wise decision the millionaire next door that wants to remain a millionaire makes without second thought.

The one who is destined to never become a millionaire, but wants to appear to look like one, would do the exact opposite. He would buy the latest, most stylish furnishings on credit and have the entire area interior decorated.

You need not care whether those who enter your home like your taste in furniture. Your furniture only need be functional for you and your family.

Chapter 15

Never enough money

Do not ever begin to think you are too wealthy.

If you begin to think you have made enough money, you will become lazy. This is especially dangerous in your quest to become the millionaire next door. Keep yourself on your financial toes by always believing no amount of money is enough.

You cannot allow yourself to become comfortable with a certain amount of money.

When you begin to feel you are making real money, do not let it go to your head, develop a bad attitude and become a show off.

There will always be someone with more money than you.

Do not ignore the lawn guy working on one of the other neighbor's yards when you are taking a walk simply because you think you may make more or be worth more than him. Wave to him.

No one is impressed with someone who tries too hard to impress others with imagined wealth. It is boring.

Do not get the false notion that you are better than others. Speak to the lawn people as you pass them when you are walking your dog. You are not better than they are. Who knows, one day you might need one of those guys to cut your lawn.

You should never treat those who have less than you as inferior to you. You may be depending on them in the future.

Chapter 16
Credibility

No matter how much money you make you cannot buy credibility.

Do not try to tell others you paid more for something than you paid for it or that something you own is worth more than it is actually is.

If you do this, you lose your credibility. People are not dumb. Most people have a good general idea of what things are worth and what things sell for.

No matter how much money you make you cannot buy credibility.

You do not have to tell people what you paid for anything.

The entire world does not need to know your business, especially your financial business.

If you buy palm trees to line the driveway of your new home, you do not have to tell the nosey neighbor what you paid for the trees.

Some financial dealings are not anyone else's business, but your own.

Chapter 17
Integrity

Without integrity you have nothing.

Your integrity means everything.

You can be the wealthiest person in the world and still not have integrity. Without integrity you have nothing.

People who do business with other people want to do business with people of integrity, just as they want their friends to be people of integrity.

In all of your business dealings, you should always try to conduct yourself with integrity. If you say you are going to deliver something, do everything in your power to do just that. If you say you are going to pay someone, pay them. Do did not try to bamboozle others with hot air and a promise of gold dust. Do not over extend yourself and always try to be the kind of person other business people would want to do business with. This is why customers will return to you repeatedly.

If you conduct yourself in this manner, many years after you leave your service business people will still be calling you.

Chapter 18
Bottom line

Your bottom line is nobody's business.

Whether a person has real wealth or not, it is a bad mistake to be a showoff.

You are better off to be the millionaire in blue jeans and tennis shoes than the guy in the three-piece suit attempting to purchase something from a seller. Who do you think is going to get the better deal?

Usually the guy in the three-piece suit is simply that, a suit with no hard wealth. He is, most often than not, buying on credit. The millionaire has the luxury of dickering on the price he is willing to pay. He is not at the mercy of the seller and the lending institution to tell him whether he can afford an item at whatever high price they are willing to sell it at with an outrageous interest rate attached.

Chapter 19
Humility

It is important that you have humility where your money is concerned.

Never assume someone is worth a certain amount of money.

When you have true hard wealth, many times it is best not to call attention to that fact.

This is part of what being the millionaire next door is all about.

Most millionaires next door would rather be incognito than have their personal lives on display.

The opposite is true of those who want you to believe they have money. Everything they do is geared toward making you think they are wealthy.

When you get into multiple millions you will not have to pretend you can afford something. Those of us who know what big money is can spot the phonies a mile away.

It is much easier to keep what you have earned to yourself, because the minute those around you know you have begun to make money, there are those that cannot wait to stick their hand out.

Whether you are making a meager salary or you have managed to amass great wealth, you do not owe family or anyone anything.

The money you have earned, no matter how you have earned it, is yours. You have every right to spend it any way you wish. That does not mean you have to lend to or supplement anyone. You do not owe it to the ones around you who have been less fortunate. They will put a guilt trip on you if you allow yourself to fall for it. Do not.

You must recognize these people are a bottomless pit with no respect for how to amass wealth. Do not allow them to get inside your pockets, because they will bleed you dry.

Chapter 20
Selfishness

If you want to become a millionaire, to some extent, you will have to learn to be selfish with what you share.

You do not have to be completely selfish. Selfishness has its place when you are attempting to become and remain a millionaire.

Know the degree to which you need to be selfish, i.e., when to be selfish and when to be generous.

Do not make the mistake of thinking everything you own is yours and yours alone. You must share equally in your wealth with your spouse. Try not to use the words his, hers and mine when you describe different assets.

It is a pleasure to be with a spouse who spends money on you. When you spend money on each other it is money you have both earned. You owe it to each other not to be selfish.

You can never let your financial guard down on how much you spend on whatever you are buying.

You invite another couple to party with you and yours, because are new to the area and you need someone to guide you around town.

The girl realizes she has an opportunity to spend someone else's money and announces she wants champagne, but not just any champagne, Dom Pérignon. Her boyfriend remains in the limousine instead of going inside and offering to pay for his girlfriend's request—remember this is the girlfriend who wants Dom Pérignon.

The millionaire next door would been happy with a $30.00 bottle of White Star that is made by the same company, Moët et Chandon—that is three bottles of White Star with change left over for the cost of one bottle of Cuvée Dom Pérignon.

Next time you party, be sure you party with friends who do not care whether or not they drink a more expensive bottle of champagne.

Chapter 21
100% business partners

It is easy to spend someone else's money. Smart men and women, who are attempting to amass great wealth, do not do that to each other.

If you and your spouse function as a team, especially when it comes to spending wisely, you will always have money.

You must be 100% business partners.

How many women do you know would help their husband roof a 2,500 square foot home rather than pay roofers to do it? It might be one of the hottest, most miserable jobs that you ever tackle, but it also might leave fifteen thousand dollars in your pocket you would have paid roofers.

How many couples do you know that would spend their weekends completely and totally remodeling homes as a second income? How many couples do you know that would fence half an acre of property themselves just to save $1,000.00?

You do not need to care what others think as long as you are making money and you are not spending it unwisely. If you think you have too much prestige, you would not consider roofing your own home. You would have done what 80% of the rest of the population does that will be ranked among the poor at retirement. You would have paid roofers to do it for you. You would have hired a fencing company and thrown away $1,000.00 that instead remained in your pockets.

To-get-here you must work together.

Chapter 22
Financial status

The reason you will gain financial status is you will earn it.

You must understand the principles that enable you to become a millionaire and live them every day of your life.

Unfortunately, the majority of those around us do not understand those principles.

You need to be done with the prestige and go for the money.

In your business dealings, do not be an ingrate, do not be judgmental and do not be insecure.

The ones who show disrespect for those who are financially smart enough to become and remain solvent are merely allowing their green monster underneath to rear its head.

You have no place for it.

You will find that those who tend to be the most ungrateful are the ones the solvent ones pull out of bankruptcy. Perhaps it is because all parties involved know the solvent ones do not owe it to someone who is financially devastated to provide them with a financial way out.

Insecurity will bite you back. It will prevent you from being all you can be in business. You have to believe in yourself to be financial dynamite. You will become better with age and as the number of your business dealing increase.

Forge ahead.

Chapter 23
Insecurity

Refuse to be personal friends with anyone who talks viscously about others and anyone who spreads gossip.

This is a trait of insecurity. You do not need people like this involved in your business or personal life. You do not want the entire world to know your personal or financial business. These are the types of people that due to their jealousy will deliberately circumvent you from becoming wealthy or wealthier if they can. These are the petty people you want to avoid like the plague.

They will bring nothing to your future financial plate, but a pea-green hunger and a wickedly jealous thirst for your wealth.

Chapter 24
Education

The wonderful thing about learning to make money is that once you know how to make money, you can always make money.

It is an education no one can take away from you.

Millionaires lose their millions one year only to be back at millionaire status a mere year or two afterwards.

You have probably been thinking you were going to get a lesson on how to make money in real estate. Wrong.

No two millionaires have made their money in the same manner. Millionaires make money in every business avenue there can possibly be.

It is not how you make your money. To a certain extent it is not even how much money you make. It is how you spend it. Even millionaires can spend themselves broke.

There is tremendous opportunity in the real estate business.

Why sell bacon and eggs when you can be selling steak?

The point is that the profit margin for steak is much higher than the profit margin for bacon and eggs.

Chapter 25
Where the money is

If you are going to spend your time doing anything to make money, whether it is buying and selling or working for a wage, go where the big money is if you want to become a millionaire.

You do not want to be poor and angry when you are too old to work. That means you must plan early not to be poor. You only have a certain number of earning years in your life. Are you going to spend your entire life working for minimum wage or are you going to wake up and go after the big dollars?

Price is everything and that also includes the price you are willing to accept as your wage.

Whether you are working for someone else or yourself, the goal is to make as much money as you can make. Why flip burgers at minimum wage if you can be laying pipe at a plumber's union wages? Why sell cars when you can sell real estate at a higher profit? Why work for the business owner for a small wage when you can own the business yourself and reap all the profits?

You wonder why the average businessman does not want to pay higher wages.

One percent of our population provides the jobs in this country and that one percent is taxed heavier than any other tax-paying group.

Our government takes so much away in taxes from those of us who make money and provide jobs that we would rather not work our money in this country. We are well aware that we do not have to bring our money into the country. Therefore, many wealthy Americans do not bring their money and/or their jobs into our country.

Our government desperately needs to get its hands out of the rich man's pockets and tax us all fairly and equally. We business owners have been stripped of our incentives to provide jobs in this country. We are taxed beyond the call of acceptability.

As long as this continues much of the money that should be in Americans pockets will not be there.

Over the past forty years, the cost of living has risen 479% according to the consumer price index, which measures the cost of living. In 1960 $173,000 was the equivalent of one million today. It will cost $5.8 million dollars in today's money to purchase what one million purchased forty years ago.

Chapter 26
Attitude

Do not have a bad attitude, the attitude that business owners owe you something.

The day that you take on the tremendous responsibility of owning the business yourself will be the day you are entitled to the profits, if there are any.

You may have to go without paychecks while your employees are paid wages for inferior labor and days they did not even bother to show up. You may have to take home minimum wage paychecks, if you take home any wages at all, while your employees receive wages well above average for their expertise, or lack of, in the area where they were working.

You may have to pay your employees and not pay yourself simply because you cannot afford to take a paycheck and keep the company afloat. You may drive a beat-up truck with no power steering and no air conditioning while your employees drive new cars far nicer than your vehicle.

That sacrifice is part of the cost of doing business in becoming the millionaire next door.

Chapter 27

College

Do the math before you go to college.

Some people have the mistaken notion that if they do not go to college, they will never become wealthy. This is not always true.

These are usually the people that are striving just to make a living. They do not actually have their sights set on becoming millionaires in their lifetime. They do not believe they can become millionaires is the reason they do not set their sights on that goal.

You must believe you can become a millionaire.

Many millionaires do not have a college education. Most of them made their money as entrepreneurs.

Two high school dropouts in a garage started Microsoft.

You can earn a master's education and still wind up working for $30,000.00 a year. It is hardly what a person with a master's degree should be earning. A college education does not necessarily mean you will make more money.

Smell the reality. This is what happens to college educated idiots who go to school to become nothing.

Do not go to college to become nothing.

If you go to college you need to go for some sort of degree that will enable you to make more money than the average Joe on the street or do not bother to go to college at all. If you are going to go to college, go to become a doctor, a lawyer, a pharmacist or a nurse. Go for something that will ensure you can make better money. Do not go to study general studies. You will walk out of college with a degree to make minimum wage like your high school graduate peers who now have four years seniority on you in the workplace. Yaouch! That is a harsh reality.

Decide what you are going to college to become and why. Have a friend set up appointments with friends of people that are in the type of job you think you might want to go to college for. Go into the meetings to ask each one of them what it is they do for a living, how much money they make and what it would take in the way of schooling to become one of them. After you come out of the meetings you should have a better idea of what it is you want to pursue via a college education.

Not all medical doctors step out of medical school into their first job making $220,000.00 a year.

A hair transplant doctor can be a true craftsman at his trade. He can be one of the best in his business and he will still make less than an eye surgeon. The hair transplant doctor can only perform one surgery a day in his own outpatient facility at approximately $4,000.00 a day.

Click those figures in your mind and you should be able to come up with a fairly close figure of what this type of doctor makes for a living in a year's time if he works every work day. It can be a decent living, but he will not be one of the doctors making a killer living like some of the eye surgeons who become multi-millionaires performing $2,500.00 eye surgeries every fifteen minutes on many patients in one day.

The hair transplant doctor can still become the millionaire next door by being smart enough to be conservative with the money he makes and wise enough not to be a show off. It will simply take the hair transplant doctor longer to become a millionaire than it will take the eye surgeon.

Chapter 28
Mechanics

Never trust an auto mechanic.

If you are capable try to do most repairs yourself if you are not yet at the point in your financial picture where you can afford to have someone work on your car. If your financial picture allows you to use a mechanic with good conscience, then have a mechanic repair your vehicle for you, but never trust a mechanic.

You may have to repair your vehicles for years before the day you feel your financial picture is bright enough that you can in good conscience have the work done on your vehicles when they break down. No one wants to be up to their elbows in grease worrying with a broken-down vehicle when there are more important things to be done like making money.

You need to be knowledgeable enough not to be bamboozled by an auto mechanic trying to get one over fast on you by over charging you and/or recommending more repair work than is necessary.

Get a second or third opinion if possible on mechanical work that needs to be done.

Chapter 29
Classic cars

If you are mechanically capable of keeping a car running on your own, classic cars make a wise investment.

Any car that is considered a classic can be insured under classic car insurance which is tremendously cheaper than insurance you pay on new model cars. Classic car insurance is sometimes less than half what you would pay for insurance on a new model car and as of the 2007 sells for as little as $98.00 a year.

Any car that is a classic has also lost its initial drop in price and will only go up in value the longer you keep it especially if you take excellent care of it.

If you can pay cash for a classic car, you are in the driver's seat to becoming the millionaire next door.

As long as you take care of a classic car, it will do nothing but appreciate.

A classic car is a good investment whether it is bought to be a driver or not.

If you buy a classic car as an investment, it is best if you choose not to drive it.

It is trivial and unimportant to show off anything you invest your money in.

One of the biggest mistakes that will keep you from becoming the millionaire next door is to have to show off everything you own.

A classic car is an investment. The more it is driven the less it is worth. If you drive the classic car to show off, in the interim you will rag it out until it is worth absolutely nothing.

It must be insignificant to you that anyone is aware that you own such a car. All you need to be concerned about is that it goes up in value.

That is the thinking of the millionaire next door. The millionaire next door is not trying to impress you. The millionaire next door is amassing wealth for his own comfort and financial sanity.

This is how you need to conduct yourself concerning the things and areas where you make your investments.

Chapter 30
Food

Food is not an investment.

Food is a need purchase.

It is an area where you have to spend your money. You simply cannot get around not eating, yet you will never receive a penny back from the money you spend on food.

It is also the area where you can waste a tremendous amount of money. Do not use food buying as an excuse to burn money.

Spend a dollar extra per pound at ten pounds a week on meat for your household and you have overspent $520.00 in one year. Add that up over thirty years and you have overspent $15,600.

You sit there a minute and think about what you could do with $15,600 if you had it in cash in your pocket today. The most expensive cut of beef does not look nearly as good as $15,600 in cash.

Which would you rather have?

The money.

Do not serve a beautiful spread of lobster, jumbo shrimp, and other expensive shellfish, enough to feed fifteen people with food left over, when you do not have the money to pay for the meal. It is not important that you show off in front of others by hosting an extravagant meal that you cannot afford. The meal can be just as excellent and your guests will be just as happy with spaghetti. Furthermore, if you can not afford to entertain don't entertain.

Do not whittle away your life savings by not concentrating on making your food dollar stretch as far as you can stretch it.

It is no wonder some people have hard financial times.

Do not buy the expensive cuts of meat, buy outrageous prepackaged foods and basically throw away your money. Learn how to shop frugally for food and spend your money wisely.

Buy thick country-style ribs the week they are on sale at .99 a pound rather than the week they cost $4.99 a pound. You will have five times as much meat in your freezer in the long run for the same price. That is what your freezer is for—to store meat.

Watch the sales at every store to ensure that you get the best price on meat.

Drive where you can purchase quality food. Know your butcher. Ask the butcher what is on sale at the best price.

You can easily do a lousy job of shopping for groceries from a financial standpoint if you do not shop conservatively and know where the deals are.

You pay yourself in the money you save when you make a point of knowing the price of foods and buying where and when you can get the best price.

The manner in which you spend your money can be the sole reason why you have an empty refrigerator and/or freezer.

Prepackaged goods are not a deal.

You see the prepackaged food gimmick almost everywhere you turn in the grocery stores. You have to hone your mind-sight in on these gimmicks and try to get around wasting your money in this manner. It is easy not to realize where and how you are wasting your grocery money, because we have become consumers of the advertisers.

Prepackaged five-ounce yellow rice that sells for eighty-eight cents is too expensive.

Okay, you snickered because it was only eighty-eight cents and you are thinking anyone can afford eighty-eight cents. You are right. Just about anyone can afford eighty-eight cents.

Use a calculator and discover what a terrible buy that eighty-eight cents prepackaged five-ounce container of yellow rice turns out to be in the long run. You can purchase five pounds of rice for ninety-nine cents, a $2.00 container of yellow Amarillo seasoning, and a forty-four cents package of salt. For a total price of $2.55, you can have five pounds of yellow rice if you are willing to season the rice yourself. If you purchase it for eighty-eight cents prepackaged at five ounces, you are spending $1.76 an ounce as opposed to thirty-one cents an ounce you would pay if you made yellow rice yourself.

Prepackaged five pounds of yellow rice costs $8.80. Not prepackaged it costs $2.55 cents. That is a difference of $6.25.

If you were to serve prepackaged yellow rice 365 days out of the year, you would have spent $321.20; times thirty years, a whopping $9,636.00. On the other hand, if you make the rice yourself every day for a year, you would have spent $113.15 in one year; times thirty years, $3,394.50. In thirty years' time the difference between what you can spend on prepackaged yellow rice at $9,636.00 and non-prepackaged yellow rice at $3,394.50 is $6,241.50.

Think of all the different ways you can spend $6,241.50 in your lifetime.

The same principle applies to baked goods. You can buy cakes already baked in the bakery if you want to throw your money away on a simple luxury in the same way you could throw your money away on prepackaged yellow rice. You should know the financial fallacy of purchasing baked goods vs. baking from scratch.

Do not convince yourself that you do not have time to bake a cake. If you are in the kitchen cooking anything, you have the time to throw a cake in the oven and let it cook while you are preparing the rest of the meal. The key is to start the cake first and let it cook while you are working.

Not only will you save money if you start baking from scratch, but you will also wind up with a much fresher product.

Who does not love fresh cake hot from the oven especially warm cake with melted butter?

Do not forgo saving money because you are too proud to buy right.

Chapter 31
Instant gratification

We have become a society that thrives on instant gratification and stands just shy of the doorway labeled poverty.

People who want instant gratification make such a monumental monetary mistake.

Instant gratification is known as credit cards, mortgages, leases, second mortgages, high dollar specialty foods, luxury items and fancy homes.

Our society as a whole has not been taught financial self-restraint. Instead the average person has bought into the belief that credit is real wealth and it is never necessary to outright own anything of value.

The truth is our society as a whole does not even begin to understand what is of value and because of that, we are not a solvent society and never will be.

Many are brainwashed into believing that it is cool to brag when they have over paid for an item. It is the mindset that the more you pay for it, the more it is worth. Like designer dinnerware at $110.00 a setting is going to hold food any better than a $2.50 place setting. It is not.

Do not believe that the more you pay for something the cooler you will become or the neater it makes you. Nothing you buy or own is going to make you any different or any better than who and what you are—not even a fancy sports car, an expensive yacht or a Lear. The fact will remain after you have spent your hard-earned money on expensive items you will still be the same person. Nothing has changed. The only thing different is you have spent your money and now you have none. Go figure. How smart was that?

Not the millionaire-next-door smart.

Chapter 32
Marriage

Do not try to marry for money. Marry for love, because most millionaires do not get divorced.

How many times have we seen someone try to marry for money?

Our media hyped the game show, "Who wants to Marry a Millionaire?" Oh, pleeeaaasssee. The saddest part to it is that they were actually able to get contestants.

Most millionaires next door do not get divorced.

Divorce is one of the costliest mistakes you will ever make. If you are not in what you consider the ideal marriage, think long and hard before you opt for a divorce. One of the first things you need to realize is not one marriage is perfect. Yours is not the only marriage that is not perfect. What you have to learn to be is accepting and forgiving. Take your marriage for what it is, what it has to offer and make the most of it.

If you walk away from love for the love of money, you will be destined to be miserable forever.

Do not believe that just because someone has money, they are happy. Nothing could be farther from the truth. Some millionaires are extremely happy, some are mediocre happy, and others are completely miserable and even more miserable to live around. You would not want to be married to the grumpy millionaire that cannot find anything to be happy about.

You must know your priorities over and above money.

Do not make your priority anything, but money. Your family and the quality of your home life should come first.

Do not fall into the mistaken notion that if you become a millionaire, money will make you happy. Money does not make you happy. You make yourself happy.

Millionaires are not gods.

Millionaires are ordinary people, just like you.

You have as much right to be the millionaire next door as any other person does.

Chapter 33
Ask

You never know the bottom line until you ask.

Do not be afraid to ask for what you want.

Dare to be bold and as you become more successful you will gain great confidence.

The main point is you must ask. Do not be afraid that you may offend the seller. What do you care if you offend the seller? He has an item for sell and this is what you want to pay for it. If he does not want to sell it for the amount you are offering you can go your separate ways without punching each other in the face. That is business.

Buying and selling is business. Approach it as such, without being emotional about the bargaining process.

There are men and women that get too emotionally wrapped up in purchasing a specific home that they over purchase on the house's price. Do not do it. Houses are bricks and mortar. One is not better than the other is—the only exception you should make is whether or not you are paying the right price based on what the home is worth. Price is all that matters.

You never know the bottom line until you ask.

Chapter 34
Persistence

That which you persist in doing becomes easier to do, not that the nature of the thing has changed, but that your ability to do it has increased.

You do not have to kick yourself repeatedly because you have made bad financial decisions in the past. Simply change the future by using your increased abilities to make wiser financial decisions.

Making and acquiring money does become easier with time, but just because you make and acquire money in your lifetime, does not mean you will arrive at your senior years a millionaire.

You must use time to your advantage.

During your earning years you will experience highs and lows in your earnings. During the times that you experience great highs, you must be conservative. This is hard for the majority and precisely why many do not become millionaires.

During the low times, you must be far more conservative. If you are using time as one of the methods that your wealth will be acquired and allowed to grow, the only piece of magic that you have in your gift bag of wealth is saving as much of the money you make as you possibly can.

Americans are some of the worst monetary savers in the world.

Chapter 35

Location, location, location.

In real estate location can be mean everything.

How many times have you heard this statement when it comes to real estate?

In real estate location does mean everything.

This does not mean only in the resale value of the real estate itself, but how far you have to travel and whether your children are going to be in better schools, etc. It can mean a host of details you never thought of, like whether or not the airport is going to annex the property within the next nine months to ten years. Or if you are going to still have riparian rights to the water when the planned road goes through your property splitting you off from your view of the water. Or if you are going to be able to retain the gas and mineral rights as the owner of the largest tract of property under which a main gas line runs. Or if you purchase ten acres of tree farm to be divided into ten one-acre tracts will you be able to do so based on the amount of road frontage you have vs. easement. And, while you are thinking about it, will the trees be included in the sale of the tree farm property?

You may move to place your child in a better A-rated school system.

If your home is too far from your work you may waste precious hours in unnecessary drive time and extra fuel cost. Every minute you are in your vehicle driving is wasted time and, yes, it is true, time is money.

The location where you live can have a significant effect on your finances.

It is important to consider carefully where you will put down roots. Once you have established yourself it is hard to pull up and move. Also, if you choose the wrong location it could cost you more than it would help you in getting ahead.

Small communities are notorious for costing you beyond belief on ridiculous items that in any other area would be plentiful at a fraction of the cost. When an area has many people, the seller has to work harder for your dollar. Therefore, competition keeps the prices down and your spending power is much greater. You may be paying slightly more taxes to live in a bigger city, but in the long run you will come out ahead.

In some of the smaller communities, you are still dealing with perhaps one car dealership that has no competition. If you are living out in the country where taxes are cheaper, you are spending your dollars in pricey gasoline and even more expensive, unproductive travel time.

Smaller communities keep pay scales lower than larger communities. Business owners that provide jobs know work is scarce. They deliberately pay below the national average simply because they can get away with it. They know too much about the individual worker in their own community, like just how desperate the worker is for work and how cheap the worker will work simply to keep food in their mouth.

Chapter 36
Too good

Do not think you are too good.

You can be one of the wealthiest in your community, wear white suits and drive a Rolls Royce and you still will not be admired greatly unless you know how to handle your finances.

There is nothing wrong with going through potential purchases item-by-item that are on sale until you decide what it is you are going to buy because it was going at a good price. You may not have to purchase anything that is on sale. You may get to the point you can buy out the entire establishment if you so desired. But not acting too proud in knowing how to handle your finances is the nature of the multi-millionaire.

This thrifty behavior is how the millionaire next door stays wealthy.

Chapter 37
Other people's opinions

Do not worry for one iota of a second what other people think of you and do not be a gossip.

No one loves a gossip. Gossips are some of the most despised people on the planet. People will be nice to a gossip's face, but what they impart behind that person's back is an entirely different picture. Unfortunately, that is why many gossips never realize what people honestly think of them and they continue their viscous cycle of gossiping. It is too bad for them.

It is best that if you cannot say something nice do not say anything at all.

You do not want to appear to act sanctimonious if you want to help others not to be judgmental. There is enough cruelty in the world without our contributing to it.

We need to uplift each other.

Anything that is negative in your life diminishes the quality of your life.

That is why it is important to forgive others. It is more for you than for the person who is forgiven. If you do not forgive, it will leave a hole in the soul. You do not always know what burdens others are carrying, but if you can see past others faults you can then be kind to yourself and feel at peace with yourself.

We are all in some ways interconnected with each other.

You know the saying "Everything that goes around comes around?" Well, there is a wiser parallel saying which is "Cast your bread on the water and it will come back buttered."

Why worry about vengeance on others? We are what we think and it is not productive to dwell on negative thoughts.

Others cannot impact our thinking in a negative way unless we allow it to happen.

To be a millionaire in our emotional lives we must let go of petty differences.

Chapter 38
Respect

Showing disrespect for another could be the one mistake that prevents you from attaining your goal to be a millionaire.

Do not be disrespectful.

The very person you disrespect may be the person you need to help you in attaining your goal to become the millionaire next door.

You should not be surprised to find that it is actually a producer's financial world. Male or female does not matter, as long as the producer makes money.

So often people are disrespectful of others. Do not make this mistake. It could be the one mistake that prevents you from attaining your goal to be a millionaire.

Show disrespect and you will get disrespect back. It is that simple.

You may find that you have to toss a few disrespectful people out of your life. Do not hesitate. Do not be afraid to tell an acquaintance to leave you alone. The quicker you get rid of them the better. If they are disrespectful to you, they are disrespectful to others and you do not need them.

Do not be a disrespectful employee.

Do not be angry that your employer is making you do a job you do not want to do. Do not be angry that you are not in your employer's position, angry because your employer requires that you not smoke near solvents, angry because your employer needs you to work late to get an order out or angry because your employer asks you to please, pick up something on your way into work. This type of anger has no value in your life.

Show your employer complete respect. When your employer pays you over time, show your appreciation with a heartfelt thank you. If you are paid extra money for the holidays, tell your employee how much it means to you. Your employee does not have to pay you anything for the holidays. If your employer gives you a raise say thank you genuinely even if it is less than what you were hoping for. This is being respectful.

In reality, you should be thankful as all get out to have a job. If you have any idea what it takes out of a business owner to provide you a job, you would know how important it is that you show your appreciation.

No business owner owes you a job. If your employer asks you to stay late to get a job out, stay late. Tomorrow you may not have a job, because if your employer's contract said he would deliver on a certain date and you do not deliver, nobody gets paid. That means no job.

Just get the job done with a respectful attitude. It makes your employer's job as business owner much easier. Here is the key. It also makes your employer much more inclined to paying you a higher wage.

Respect for an employer earns a higher wage.

A higher wage means more money to be saved and a faster road to becoming the millionaire next door.

Chapter 39
Spending habits

Revamp your spending habits.

You cannot spend all of your free time in the mall spending money. Malls are overpriced with nothing worthwhile to buy. Mall business owners pay exorbitant rents and they pass that cost on to the consumer in high prices. Malls are not where you should choose to spend your money.

You have to show respect for your money and the manner in which it is earned by not spending it frivolously.

If your husband works seven days a week so you can take care of your family, you do not go to the mall and buy yourself an eight carat diamond bracelet one week and an expensive white gold bracelet the next on your mutual credit card. You do not attempt to cajole your husband into putting an addition on the house by accidentally-on-purpose getting pregnant a third time after he has explained repeatedly you could not afford an addition to your home.

If you function with a spend-spend mentality, you will be placing a financial burden on your household that you may never be able to get out from underneath.

Less is best.

You do not need all the things you want to buy. You need to start thinking more about where and how you spend your money. You need to think about retirement and how your youthful ability to do the work you are doing will diminish in time. You need to be wise and pull back from spending.

If you do not, you may spend to the point you can not keep up.

If you are patient and spend your money wisely, one day you will realize you are the millionaire next door.

You may be living in a house you and your spouse bought when it was just the two of you and a dog. Since then you have had two children and the home is small, but comfortable and it will be paid for in two years. You would like to buy a bigger home.

Do not do it until you can pay cash for the larger home.

Sit tight, pay off your smaller home, and save your money for a larger home.

Some millionaires do not realize they are rich until they pay cash for a 1.5 million-dollar yacht or write a 500 thousand dollar check for a used helicopter.

This will happen to you if you wait to pay cash for the home of your dreams and all of your "want" purchases.

Chapter 40
Pride

Lose the pride.

You may suddenly inherit a large sum of money.

Do not quit your day job.

Do not let your pride get in the way and try to make everyone think you inherited much more than you did even if it is enough that you are able to build a house and not work for a brief period.

You will not have earned your newfound money. You may not understand what it took to make it. You may not understand what it will take to keep it and make it grow under your care. If you have never been in business for yourself, you may be destined to fail at maintaining your inheritance.

If you buy ten acres of property in an area of town where you have to drive down a street of trailer houses to get to your new home, you have already made a location error. Anyone who understood how important location is would not have chosen to build an expensive home in an area of trailer homes. If you build a large three-story home and start a horse farm because you love horses, you will be doomed since horse farms very rarely make any real money.

You simply may not be a businessperson.

You may soon find that your inheritance can dwindle fast.

The time of inheritance is the time to construct good sound financial footing. You do not want your friends betting on how fast you will spend yourself broke. It is time for a non-arrogant appearance about how much money you have. It is not the time to purchase a brand-new wardrobe of clothes, shoes, and household items on a daily basis. If you do this you are being irresponsible and you will spend yourself broke.

Eventually you will have to go back to work with a lot less ego attached and sell the home you are unable to maintain.

The newly inherited rich are almost always clueless when it comes to how to make money and how to keep it.

Chapter 41
Choices

Your financial bottom line is determined almost solely by the choices you make.

You could be the heir who decides to spend money on cocaine, a losing proposition horse farm and tons of worthless clothing.

You could decide to do nothing at all or you could seek well paying ways to make money.

Your financial bottom line is your own choice. There are many different ways to make money.

If you want to be the millionaire next door, you need make the conscientious choice to seek well paying ways to make money and maintain the money you do have like it was your last penny.

Chapter 42
Seduction

Do not be seduced by money.

You say you want to be a millionaire no matter what the cost. Do not be too anxious to jump in the fire and be careful of what you wish for. It is easy to be seduced by money and lose yourself in the interim.

Do not allow another people's opinion affect how you feel about yourself.

You do not need another person's opinion to determine who you are or how you should act.

People tend to be critical, hypocritical and self-righteous. As a result, they are hurtful. They harp on what you drive, how you eat, what you wear, etc. They even go so far to suggest you change, because they do not like you just the way you are. Do not allow them to get you wrapped up.

As long as you are living right, allow yourself the freedom to be who you are and behave in the manner that you feel most comfortable. No matter how you act or how you represent yourself, you will always have those who will have a difference of opinion.

Chapter 43
Respect

Learn to show respect for every person's individualities and teach others that you expect them to grow up and do the same.

You should know who you are and not pretend to be something that you are not.

Do not subject others to your negative feelings. People do not lose those memories.

The minute you cease striving to make everyone else happy at your expense, you discover it is much easier to make yourself happy and concentrate on the areas you need to focus on in order to make yourself the millionaire next door.

People, as a whole, absolutely love people who are genuine.

People amazingly gravitate toward those of us who are genuine and are not afraid to show we have a style of our own.

People respect people who respect themselves.

If you are concerned what the neighbor who drives a brand-new Porsche slope nose will think of you because you drive a ten-year-old Ford truck. Do not be. Be content to know your ten-year-old Ford is paid for. His Porsche is more than likely not paid for. It is not important that you show off your wealth.

You can double your money by folding it in half and putting it back in your pocket.

Those driving the Porsche are not doubling their money. They are not spending wisely when they pay the high cost of insurance in order to insure such an expensive sports car.

Those who are concerned about what others will think about them are the ones who are driving the financed or leased expensive sports cars. It is a form of insecurity.

How many times have you heard the saying that a guy's fine sporty car is an extension of his masculinity?

The millionaire next door that has money in the bank does not care whether or not his car is new or ten-years-old, because he does not have to have an extension of his masculinity. He is not so insecure that cars are the only thing he can think about and talk about. He does not lust after the frivolous. He can take it or leave it without thinking less of himself as a person.

The millionaire next door's mentality is more concerned with how much money is in the bank than how much money he is driving on the street. It is the other people on the street which have a problem. Their problem is with what everyone else is driving and it is exactly that, their problem.

The millionaire next door does not have a problem. He has money in the bank, the ability to buy any car he wanted if he so desired and he is smart enough not to be dumb with the way he spends his money.

Chapter 44
Shop slowly

Shopping slowly will help you decide whether or not you want to spend your money on an item. It will save you from overspending.

You find a two-year-old Jaguar on the showroom floor that you decide to purchase. Your truck has blown its engine and you need a vehicle. You dicker on the price with the dealership and finally come down to a $2,000.00 difference.

Based on the price of the car, $2,000.00 is not a tremendous amount of money. Yet the longer the dealership lets you think about how much you are paying for a Jaguar, the less you should want to spend that kind of money.

You love the car. You want to buy it. Instead, you should begin to mull over the thought that you are spending a lot of money because it is Jaguar. You know you can buy a different model car with all the same features for less money. This is the car you will be driving, but it should not be important to you that you drive a more expensive Jaguar or a lesser expensive different model car. What does matter is how much you spend on a car.

Think of the ways you could invest and use the money and before long, you should be deciding that you do not want to spend that kind of money on a Jaguar. If you pass on buying the car, within a month you may find a two-year-old fully loaded Lincoln Continental for half the price of the Jaguar.

Most people would take a Jaguar over a Lincoln Continental.

Those same people are not the people who will become the millionaire next door.

It all boils down to the price tag.

Use the principle of shopping slowly with even smaller purchases. Try to be sure that you have time to think about what you are considering buying. Put potential purchases in your cart and shop around the store for a while before you head to the cash register. You may wind up deciding against something and put it back.

Shopping slowly will help you to decide whether or not you want to spend your money on each and every item. It will save you repeatedly from overspending and the bothersome task of returning.

Chapter 45
Junk

Do not collect invaluable junk.

This is exactly what you are doing when you purchase $50.00 worth of Christmas decorations you do not need. It is a good example of how easily money can be thrown away with nothing to show for it.

People collect all kinds of crazy nonsense with the idea that they are collecting something worth having. It can be stuffed animals, figurines, glassware, baseball cards, etc. You name it.

Do not believe the collector of a certain brand of collectable teddy bears will amass a collection that will become her daughter's college fund, because that is exactly where that college fund is going to stay—in the form of stuffed teddy bears.

Sadly enough, collecting collectable things will not make you a millionaire.

Do not buy a Harley Davidson motorcycle replica of a collector's edition bike for $135.00 just because it looks like your Harley Davidson. You can fill your house with this wasteful spending and discover you cannot get more than a dollar for any of your replicas at your moving sale.

Some things are not worth spending your money on to display in your home even if they cost ten thousand dollars.

You will begin to notice many things are merchandised today as being collectable.

Recognize what is worth buying and what is not.

Chapter 46
Value of Money

We live in a wasteful society in which few know the value of money.

Children should be taught the value of money. If they are taught at an early age to value money, then they will take that with them into their adulthood. You cannot give a child a better gift than teaching the value of every dollar.

If a child understands that $100.00 is a ridiculous amount of money to pay for a pair of tennis shoes just because that shoe's brand name has been merchandised well, he will be a better money manager because of it. Perhaps he will grow up to merchandise and manufacture his own brand of tennis shoe to sell to all those who fall for expensive well-merchandised brands.

If you are a runner and you purchase $75.00 name brand tennis shoes that literally fall off your feet after three months, you have not gotten a good deal for your money. On the other hand, if you buy a $10.99 pair of quality tennis shoes and they last a year of running wear and tear, you have gotten a good deal for your money.

Your child goes away on a field trip for five days and takes twenty dollars a day spending money in cash. Your child returns home with $97.35. You ask why and your child explains that all the other kids spent their money on a forty-dollar singing cat and a host of other junk at the gift shops, but your child saw the things as "overpriced junk" and "a waste of money." Your child was the only child with money by the end of the trip and all of the other kids were trying to borrow money from your child.

You can be rightfully proud.

You have taught your child well and witnessed your child at the beginning stages of possibly becoming a millionaire.

Chapter 47
Credit

If you have buried yourself in credit, get credit counseling.

You will never amass wealth if you remain buried in credit and continue to abuse your ability to use credit. You can prevent yourself from becoming wealthy by spending before you make it. Interest rates on credit cards are exorbitant. Using credit cards is a losing situation.

If your spouse is abusing your credit, you may have to take your credit cards away from your spouse. There are cards that are set up so that there is a set limit that might be the solution to preventing your spouse from overspending.

If you are the one abusing your own credit, you may have to cut up and cancel your own cards. It will be the best thing you ever did for yourself financially.

When you begin to roll into bigger financial opportunities, there will be times your credit will matter to those you do business with.

You may suddenly find yourself traveling internationally. As a result your Platinum American Express can become upward twenty thousand dollars for one month. Can you imagine trying to travel out of the country to do business carrying twenty thousand in cash? It is not a safe, smart way to travel.

As a business owner if you are ordering supplies that are to be paid within thirty days, the supplier will want to check your credit. If you have been financially responsible with others who have lent you credit, suppliers feel you will treat them the same way. They are more apt to lend credit to those who pay their bills.

Now you wonder why, if you are solvent, do you need any credit.

It is called floating on someone else's money. Why would you want to spend $20,000.00 cash on stainless steel 4X8 sheets, when the supplier is willing to let you wait thirty days to pay for it without charging interest? During that thirty-day period, you may need that

$20,000.00 to pay your employees salaries. You may need other supplies that suppliers are not willing to drop ship on credit.

Also, during that thirty-day period, the business may be able to get the $1,000,000.00 job out that the stainless-steel sheets were purchased for and be paid in the interim. Now instead of having $20,000.00, you have $1,020,000.00 in your bank account and you owe $20,000.00 which will be paid 10 days before the due date in order to get a 1.5% credit off the purchase price of $20,000.00 offered by the supplier to insure creditors pay timely. That is a saving of $300.00.

Chapter 48

Financial stability

Doing business with people of means you will discover the importance of financial stability.

Bankers who own the banks are some of the richest people in the world. Some billionaires buy banks for the fun of it.

There is no doubt these are the people with the money. They recognize the letter of the law when it comes to contracts, they pay according to their contracts and they want to do business with people who are solvent. The first thing the owners of the banks do when you have approached them to do business, such as sell them a two-million-dollar job, is they check you out. If you personally are not solvent and do not have credibility, you will never be able to convince any banker to do business with you.

Financial stability will open doors for you, where all others will fail due to nothing else but their lack of financial stability.

Chapter 49
Keep control

Never trust anyone else with your money.

You may think your money might be better off invested with someone else. Never entrust your money into the hands of anyone other than yourself. Be sure you are the only one who can sign on your accounts with the exception of your spouse, if that spouse is trustworthy.

Always keep control of your money.

You may think investing in a high paying money scheme might be the solution to getting rich quick. Do not do it.

You invest a sizeable sum of money into a Cincinnati investment company. It makes you one of the larger investors with this company. After a show of high profits on paper, you decide you need your cash and withdraw the investment amount. Four months later the stockbroker doing the investing is arrested for a Ponzi scheme. He was bringing in investors by word of mouth from all the other investors who were seeing profits on paper. In reality the stockbroker was losing money and he was using the new investors' monies to pay other investors' profits. He eventually goes to jail and his multi-millionaire partner who lost everything is absolved of doing anything wrong. The multi-millionaire partner's only crime is that he entrusted someone else with his money.

You pulled your money out just in time. But what if you had not? Most of the investors who left their money in the company lost every cent when the news hit.

You managed to be lucky, but next time you might not be so lucky.

Once you lose a huge investment it is extremely hard to recoup.

If you have money you would like to invest, place it an area where you can be in control and make certain that all money made off that investment goes directly into your hands.

As you age, you are unable to physically exert yourself like you did when you were younger. Investments need to require little if any labor. A good retirement investment is in commercial real estate. Commercial renters are required to maintain the building, pay the taxes and your lease amount. This can be a large sum of monthly income for a retiree if the building is paid for at retirement.

Chapter 50
Desire

In order to become the millionaire next door, you have to have the desire.

You may have had the desire all of your life not to be poor and to become wealthy. Having the desire to become the millionaire next door runs hand in hand with setting the goal to becoming the millionaire next door. Without the desire, you will never set the goal and attain it.

But if you have the desire and you set the goal to become the millionaire next door, you will achieve it.

You may have always wanted a Mercedes. You envision yourself driving a red four-door fully loaded top-of-the-line series sedan. This vision is part of the reason that you work as hard as you do. You hope that the day will come that you will be able to afford your dream car. The day you realize you can afford to purchase your dream car is the day you realize you don't really want it. It was the fact that you thought you could never afford one that you focused yourself on doing the things necessary to attain it. Without the vision, you would not have had something to work toward.

Raise your awareness, level your sight and envision yourself as the millionaire next door.

The attainment of that goal will follow.

Chapter 51

Sex drive

The wealthiest, more successful people also have the strongest sex drives.

If you find you have a low sex drive, you may want to see a doctor about increasing your sex drive. Without a strong sex drive, you will have low motivation that will interfere with the attainment of your monetary goals. If you have a strong sex drive, it will roll over into your ability to work harder and give you the added advantage of stamina.

Attaining wealth is one area where your health can mean everything to you.

You may have to work double shifts. If you do not stay in good health you will not be able to do what it takes to stay afloat. If you have stamina, you will be able to do what it takes to stay ahead of the financial war game.

Exercise and eat right solely for the goal of maintaining stamina.

Your attainment of becoming a millionaire may depend on how healthy you are.

Chapter 52
Believe

Do not hold yourself back because you do not believe you can become a millionaire.

You have to believe you can. If you do not believe you can become a millionaire, you will not achieve the goal. You will have prevented yourself from being successful because you believe yourself to be a loser.

Believe yourself to be a loser and you will be a loser. Believe yourself to be a winner and you will be a winner. Believe you can become a millionaire and you will become a millionaire.

This is the time where you have to make the decision to take charge and be in command of your life. It means you have to make yourself a figurehead in the world of work. Even if it means you alone will be the only responsible one around you. That is okay. You continue to work today, placing stock in you, your own personal corporation.

Yesterday you had a plan to become the millionaire next door. Today you will put that plan into action. Every day for the rest of your life you will contribute something to becoming the millionaire next door and you will wait patiently until the sum of the days brings you success.

This means you will practice self-control. You will exude enthusiasm. You will be unselfish and you will sacrifice your time and energy toward this means.

Anything worth doing is worth doing right.

If you cannot do it right, don't bother. You will get back what you give, so if you want quality, give quality. If you want good payment for a job, do a good job equal to the payment.

Chapter 53

Crabs in a bucket

Most of us have had to deal with people and will have to deal with people who will do anything they can to make certain they prevent you from getting ahead. It is like being a crab in a bucket of crabs.

The minute a crab gets a hold of the edge of the bucket and begins to pull out of the bucket to freedom, the other crabs in the bucket grab him and pull him back inside the bucket.

It appears the majority of people are crabs in a bucket pinching at you, yanking you back in the bucket, hissing that you cannot get out of the bucket no matter how hard you try, that you are one of them, just another crab in a bucket full of crabs.

Do not believe it.

The significant difference is there are those of us who do manage to crawl out of that bucket due to no help from the other crabs. When you are one of the crabs in the bucket, you cannot see the crab that has managed to get out of the bucket, because you are too busy dealing with crawling out from underneath other crabs. There are so many crabs in the bucket that the other crabs have trouble noticing those of us who have been standing outside of the bucket for a very long time.

When you are on the outside looking in, suddenly it becomes crystal clear that you do not ever want to be one of those crabs in the bucket. You would rather cut claws off to save your hide from being in that bucket full of greedy crabs. The minute you realize this, your perception changes drastically and it becomes easier to snap the claw off any crab that would hold you back or prevent you from getting ahead.

Once you have been able to identify the world as a bucket full of crabs with a select few crabs that have gained freedom, you realize which crabs you would rather hang out with.

There are few people in this world that will make a difference in your life.

Be sure you identify them early on and attach yourself to them in any way you can. Rather than being crabs in a bucket, these are the people who work miracles for others because of their examples, kind acts, giving ways and teaching nature. These are the people that will change your life for the better. This person might be the mentor that helps you be promoted within your workplace or the teacher that challenges you to do your best. It may be the man or woman that makes certain you get your million-dollar proposal signed into a viable contract.

You never know whom that person may be that makes a significant change in your life, but once you have had one of these people make a difference in your life, be sure that you never leave that circle of giving unbroken.

If you reach back inside the bucket and pull one crab out of the bucket to safety, then you have done your part.

Chapter 54
Prejudice

Do not be prejudiced.

We are a global business community. You will need to be accepting and get along with all types of people. Do it genuinely.

This also includes losing your prejudices toward religion and sexual preferences.

Imagine yourself as that one different person in a world of hatred every time you start to judge another for their differences and stop yourself from continuing a cycle of hatred. You are not in junior high anymore. You are in the real world. Instead put your hand out in acceptance and allow your openness to bring you the mother lode of friendship, wealth and business across the world.

No one person's dollar is any greener that the next person's dollar.

If you want to get ahead in the financial world, you will need to study and open your eyes and heart to cultures other than what you consider your own. The world is a global marketplace, not My-town, Where-I-was-born, USA.

Business is for the betterment of everyone.

Do not listen to what grand pop taught you about segregation and what he thought about it. Form your own opinion. Do not carry on World War II hatred, because your father fought in the war and will not let you forget his anger. Start today to erase any preconceived prejudices you may have and forget your religious trappings.

It will take our global resources and peaceful cooperation to grow and survive. You are not alone in this world and you must be willing to take the handshake of the man or woman across the globe that extends a hand.

Host an exchange student.

Your child might form a lasting friendship and may eventually do business across the globe with that child.

Whatever you do, start to see the big picture—the global picture.

Chapter 55

Within your means

Do not live above your means.

Many of the people that live rich lifestyles live paycheck to paycheck and significantly far above their means. This is a terrible lifetime mistake, yet you see it among most of the so-called wealthy in our society.

Whether you think $50,000.00 a year is a lot of money or if you think $250,000.00 a year is more what you consider to be a wealthy person's annual income, does not matter.

You asked how to become the millionaire next door, not how to become the billionaire next door, so this is in keeping within that monetary perimeter. If you want to become a billionaire, buy banks when you become a multi-millionaire.

Neither $50,000.00 nor $250,000.00 is a huge yearly income. You can become a millionaire based on either income, well below the first figure, in between those two figures, and above the latter figure.

Becoming the millionaire next door has to more do with how you spend, not necessarily how much money you make.

If you want to be wealthy, you have to learn to live within your income whatever it may be.

You are a television personality that makes $250,000.00 a year. Your contract is signed for four years which means that within that time frame your income will be one million dollars. You spend every dime of your money looking the part of making that income during your four-year contract and then your contract is not renewed.

You have not lived within your income.

The Random house book entitled "The Tightwad Gazette" by Amy Dacyczn delves into this premise wonderfully—better than any book on the market. You can learn how to live within and far below your means. It is a book that promotes thrift as a viable lifestyle. She also has books entitled, "The Tightwad Gazette II" and "The Tightwad Gazette III."

It is all about not overspending. When you and your family have your act together and are not constantly overspending there is more chance of having peace of mind. This ultimately leads to more stability in the home. The same principles of fairness and respect that are necessary in business are also the governing rules that insure a stable home.

More businesses and marriages fail due to monetary instability.

Do not be an egotistical dreamer.

You may be destined for greatness, but live in that manner when you achieve it. Live only within what you can afford, even if it is less than how great you think you should be.

Chapter 56
Copy

Copy what someone else is doing.

You want to be told exactly what you should be doing to become the millionaire next door. Well this should not come as a shock to you. No one can do that for you. We are all different. All of our assets are different, our education, our experiences and abilities and our opportunities are no where near the same. You are the only one that can look around and assess what it is you should be doing to make you as much money as you can possibly make based on what is available to you.

You must utilize every single asset you have to your advantage. Stop looking around you and moaning about what is not right and use what is available to you.

Dr. Wayne W. Dyer does an excellent job of explaining this in his personal transformation book entitled, "You'll See it When you Believe it" published by William Morrow. You should read his book to get a better handle on this ideal mental state that will put you in the captain's seat to becoming all you can be.

Being a reader and a dreamer will never be enough to place you in the position of being the millionaire next door. You must be a doer. You must learn to work physically as well as mentally.

There are many people who are making money. You see them every day, but do you know what they actually do to make a living? Ask them. At the same time ask them all about how they got started and what it took to get off the ground, etc. Let them educate you by being inquisitive. People love to teach someone about themselves and what they do for a living.

Eventually you will come across someone who is doing something that you have all the assets available to you to copy.

Forget what you were taught in school about never copying anyone.

If someone is making money at something, you can make money by doing the same thing.

You spot a magazine in a resort town while on vacation that you know you could make big money if you copied the same type of magazine. Go back home and start a magazine just like it on your kitchen table. You may sell the business for over one hundred million dollars years later.

You see how simple it is.

There are many different businesses that you see every day in direct competition with each other, sometimes even across the street from one another. It is right in front of your eyes. Look at Walgreen vs. Eckerd, Home Depot vs. Lowes, Wal-Mart vs. Kmart.

Why would you think it would not be a good idea to copy what someone else is doing if they are making money at it—unless, of course, you are looking for excuses.

If you find an excuse for not doing anything and it is the reason you have not ventured into any sort of business venture, you will have to live with it. It is your decision.

When you seek a new business, you may consider hundreds of different businesses before you finally decide on one. There are many factors you will have to take into consideration, but one of the first prerequisites should be to consider that it already be a form of business that is a proven big money maker. It may be that you look at it for its potential to become a franchised business all over the country. You may look at its lack of competition, but mostly you should look at its profit margin.

Chapter 57
Safety and protection

Choose safety and security first by protecting your property and yourself.

Protect your assets with property casualty coverage, such as auto insurance, homeowner's insurance, renters insurance and umbrella liability. Shop for the best price on full coverage. Increase your deductible and cut your premiums by as much as twenty percent. Protect yourself with personal life and disability insurance policies.

Think twice before you go with the Bull.

Fortunately, the stock market has a duplicitous nickname which is perfect for it.

Work your money yourself in a manner in which you can maintain control where you can reap higher returns. Perhaps for you that may be in your own business or in rental property. It does not matter where. As long as it is any place no one else can take it away from you.

Fifty-three percent of American families have invested in the stock market.

If you do choose the stock market route, get solid advice from an established firm or broker and build a portfolio based on the safer, more surefire routes of investing.

Whatever you do, don't be a gambler.

Whether you are gambling in the stock market or on the roulette table, you are still gambling with your money and it is a losing proposition. Do not be enticed into the world of gambling.

If you are going to gamble, you might as well stand at the top of a New York high rise and throw every dollar bill you have in assets over the edge into the street. Whether you are gambling in Las Vegas or the stock market or tossing your money over the edge of a tall building, it is no different than getting hooked on drugs.

Chapter 58

Addictions and depression

Addictions and depression will sap your last dime.

If you battle an addition whether drug or gambling, seek help. Don't try to go it alone, but whatever you do, kick the habit. You are not expected to be perfect and you will not be able to kick the problem yourself.

Everyone has feelings of being sad and down some times which is normal.

The real psychiatric and medical illness called depression is a disorder of mood that can be severe and may be life threatening.

You could have true depression if you have experienced any five of the following nine symptoms for at least two weeks for the most of every day:

Having a very low mood.

Experiencing suicidal thoughts.

Decreased interest in activities, and little pleasure in anything, including sex.

Five percent decrease or increase in weight over about a month.

Insomnia or sleeping too much.

Fatigue or loss of energy.

Feeling guilty or worthless with no real reason.

Decreased ability to concentrate or think.

Feeling lethargic or agitated.

Unfortunately, depression runs in families. You might recognize a similar syndrome in a parent or sibling. Depression is often seen as a flaw of character and therefore goes unrecognized. This misperception can be tragic and sometimes even fatal. Depression is almost always easily treatable with a combination of therapy and medications.

Vices will destroy your dreams.

Try to become vice free.

Chapter 59

Losses

Cut your losses.

Once you have realized you have made a bad financial decision, cut your losses as soon as possible. Do not hesitate. File bankruptcy if you have to. If you have allowed yourself to sink into debt so badly that you need to file bankruptcy, then do it, because you cannot get back on track with your finances until you do.

Chapter 60

Time value vs. money value

Your time will become more valuable than your physical labor.

There will come a time in your life where you cannot afford to do certain tasks. Your time will be more valuable and you will need to hire the work to be done. When you are at this point, you don't need to be cutting the lawn, trimming the hedges, repairing your vehicles, fixing the roof, etc. Hire someone to do those tasks and put your talents to work doing the things that make you money.

Learn to take an attitude adjustment.

Don't let your past days of being in the poorhouse prevent you from realizing there is a time that you are more valuable than an hourly job you can pay to have done. Hire the work to be done and put your skills to work where they are more valued monetarily. You will have to figure out what is worth your time to do and what is not. Those tasks will also change as your financial status changes.

Chapter 61
Simplicity

You must keep it simple and keep your greed in check.

You have a responsibility to every possession you own. Keep it simple.

The simpler you keep your life the easier your life will be.

You have to think before you buy. Do not buy on a whim simply because you think it would be cool to have some gizmo you do not need. Think about the costs that will come with maintaining ownership of that item.

Most possessions are a waste of money.

Many people have the mistaken notion that a person's possessions signify how wealthy they are. This is not true. It does not signify how much cash money a person has or what their property holdings are.

Chapter 62
Greed

When they invented money, they invented greed.

You are a contractor who has been asked to give a quote on a new building a multi-millionaire is considering building. You send the quote came back at five times what the multi-millionaire could build this building for if he did it himself without the contractor. The ironic thing about your contractor's quote is that you know the multi-millionaire does not need you to build this building. It is a building he can build without any contractor, so to quote him a ridiculously high profit price is not wise, except that you know the multi-millionaire can afford to build it even if it did cost him five times the reasonable rate it should be.

Do you think the multi-millionaire would use a contractor that is flat out being greedy especially in a contractor competitive environment?

As a result, you lose the opportunity that you would have had if you had quoted reasonably in the first place. If you had only kept your greed in check and quoted where you could have made a reasonable profit, you would have had the contract.

You have a right to a profit, just not a profit that rips the skin off the teeth of your customer.

You must keep your greed in check.

Most people who are in the position to do big business with you have been around the block a few times too many and they know what they are doing, even if you do not.

There will always be someone out there who will do the job you are competing for cheaper.

Take that into consideration anytime you are trying to compete in a competitive marketplace.

You are in the lawn service business and you want to make it more profitable.

The lawn service business is a highly competitive business. You had managed to build a company as a high school teenager who talked his dad into fronting him the money for a lawnmower to quite a fleet of equipment and vehicles accompanied by a drove of workers years later.

You are not making any money, because you are working too cheap.

You must work smarter not harder.

The first thing you need to do is stop doing business with any customer that does not pay on time or gives you a bad time; thus, taking your valuable time away from more important money-making matters. All business owners have those customers that are a royal pain. It is best not to do business with them at all. Do not let them sap you of your time and energy. Let some other competitor handle that customer.

The second thing you need to do is raise your prices and lose all of your smaller customers. If you lose some customers in the interim, it will not matter. You will make up for it in the raise you give yourself when you raise your prices to the point they need to be in order for you to make a clean profit. You will be working less and making more money. Therefore, you would be working smarter not harder.

You have to take into consideration your equipment costs, maintenance, insurance, salaries, leases, etc. You have a large company, which means you cannot work as cheap as the solitary lawn care man who only has a lawnmower and a truck. You also have an advantage over the single lawn care man. You can handle the upkeep of large apartment complexes, expansive housing units and other bigger jobs.

You must sell your company on the size and quality of the job your company is able to provide.

You must be smart enough to tweak it like tuning a fine guitar without losing your entire business by being unwise enough to sky rocket your price on a very competitive business.

You must consider danger vs. safety.

You can compare this to a cat that must change his landing in midair flight because a new object has been placed in his normally empty ideal landing spot. It can be done, but it must be done delicately in order to survive the landing.

You could be in danger of losing your balanced business altogether if you are greedy in the raising of your prices. If you are not and you are reasonable, you will survive the financial landing beautifully.

Chapter 63
Business change

Maneuver yourself into a business that you understand and have some knowledge of.

You decide you want to do something different. You are tired of doing what you are doing, but you do not know what it would be that you could put your efforts into.

Assess all of the businesses that are related to your present lawn care business. You could be thinking the lawn sprinkler business, an indoor plant care business, the chemical lawn care business and the plant nursery business. Then assess any businesses that are related to the hobbies you enjoy. You would like to own a gym, but you feel the equipment is out of your financial reach.

If you are moving from one business to the next, you should try to decide on a business that is related to the one you are in so you are able to utilize the equipment and manpower you already have available at your fingertips.

You should consider any one of the four businesses that are related to your present lawn care business.

Chapter 64
Organization

Organization is everything in the game of making money.

You cannot make money if you are disorganized. At least you cannot make as much money as you would be able to make if you were in order. You need to know where things are and have a place for everything.

Lose the junk and do not keep anything that is not nice and is not functional. Functionality is an important rule of thumb on staying organized, and deciding what to keep and what to toss.

Use whatever system gets you organized and works for you.

Whether it is sticky notes or a day planner, it does not matter as long as it gets you organized so your time becomes manageable and you are able to accomplish all that you need to or can get done.

Chapter 65
Mortgage

If you must mortgage your home, do so at the best rate so you can get out of debt fast.

Realtors want to sell you the highest priced piece of property they call sell you so their commission is a large one. They have no interest in your financial well being. The way they accomplish this is to sell you the most house you can manage to pay for based on a thirty year plan so your principal and interest is low enough you can afford the payments each month. They give you examples such as the following one:

$120,000.00 for 30 years at 8 1/4% = 120

120 X 7.51 = $901.20

Payment per month will be $901.20 (Principal and interest)

What they do not tell you is when you pay off this $120,000.00 home in thirty years you will have actually paid $417,000.00 total at the end of the thirty-year period. That is the purchase price of $120,000.00 plus $297,000.00 interest. That is a lot of money thrown away in your lifetime.

The important thing you have to remember is you are only going to make so much money in your lifetime. If you have already locked yourself in to this sort of payment plan, you should consider changing it.

The difference can be significant.

If you buy the same $120,000.00 home on a fifteen-year plan at 8 1/4%, you will pay $148,000.00 in interest for a total cost of $268,000.00.

If you buy this $120,000.00 home on a ten-year plan at 8 1/4% you will pay $99,000.00 in interest for a total of $219,000.00.

The difference in the amount of your payments is not that significant.

The following shows you the amount your payment per month would be based on the different time plans:

30 years = $901.20 per month
15 years = 1,164.00 per month
10 years = 1,472.40 per month

When you consider the difference between paying $417,000.00 in thirty years and paying $219,000.00 in ten years is $198,000.00, you realize you are not being financially smart to mortgage a home based on a thirty-year timeframe. The other added advantage to a ten-year plan is you will be out of debt fast.

Chapter 66

Bottom to top

Start at the beginning not at the top.

In becoming the millionaire next door what matters is that you do what it takes to make the money even if it means selling cars for a while before you own the car lot.

Luck is a factor sometimes. You have to be in the right place at the right time even if it means starting at the bottom.

You do this by acting with wisdom not fear.

When opportunity presents itself you have to have the wisdom to proceed forward without fear as to where you are going to end up. Once you are orienting yourself in a certain direction and surrounding yourself with that environment, all of the elements will help you to succeed in the direction you are headed.

Chapter 67
Jealousy

Do not let jealousy hold you back and do not hold others back because of your jealousy.

Instead turn your jealousy around to pride and take pride in seeing your friends and loved ones succeed. Or better help them to succeed in any manner you can.

Jealousy should have no place in your life.

If you will adhere to this principle and begin to thrill at the successes of others, even shove them toward their successes with all your strength you will find it has a constructive boomerang effect.

You will find others will be there to help you reach your success much faster and easier as a result.

Chapter 68
Pace

Pace yourself.

Do not take on too much.

You cannot do too much at one time or you will burn yourself out too easily.

You cannot function at your optimum if you are tired and strung out.

Pace yourself.

Becoming the millionaire next door does not have to be a race run by the hare, you can be the tortoise and still win.

There is nothing wrong with knowing where you are going and getting there in as direct a path as you can. You do not have to run over anyone as you are getting there. You do not have to arrive exhausted.

No person's life is the same as another's life. You must customize pacing to fit your needs.

Your ultimate goal is to customize your pacing to epitomize the quality of your personal life.

If you do not pace yourself, you will not have a functional life at home or in business.

Pacing is conducive to the kind of well-balanced life that is necessary for you to be happy on the path to and at the arrival of becoming the millionaire next door.

If it is not working change your path quickly.

You have to throw a lot of mud on the wall before some of it sticks.

Believe in yourself, because you are the only person who will never let you down.

Do not doubt your ability or your potential no matter what your pace may be. You also must believe you can do anything you desire to do with unwavering doubt or you will be doomed to failure.

You are the only person you can depend on even if it takes you longer than you expected.

Chapter 69
Plan

Have a plan.

Any plan. You are the only one that knows what you are good at, where you want to end up, etc. You will have to develop a custom plan that you will cut out for yourself individually.

What is most important is that you have a plan, that you are not idly floating through life thinking you do not have to do anything to reach the goal of becoming the millionaire next door. If you are thinking you can do nothing and millions of dollars are suddenly going to pop into your bank account when you turn sixty-five, you will be waking up to a harsh reality when you get ready to retire.

Having good strong financial success is a product of good common sense.

You can become the millionaire next door when you plan and implement the methods of attaining and keeping wealth in your everyday life.

Now you know you can become the millionaire next door.

Don't miss out!

Visit the website below and you can sign up to receive emails whenever Kay Duncan publishes a new book. There's no charge and no obligation.

https://books2read.com/r/B-A-HJVRC-SLLFF

BOOKS 2 READ

Connecting independent readers to independent writers.

Did you love *How to Become the Millionaire Next Door 4th Ed.*? Then you should read *Intercell*[1] by Kay Duncan!

[2]

Cybertech's scientists perfected Smart Chip, an E-prom chip one hundred times faster than Prodigy and unlike any computer technology that we have on the market today. Cybersoft expected to revolutionize the computer industry with it and kept the technology under top secret wraps at this facility. It is unknown whether the technology was destroyed in the blaze.

---

1. https://books2read.com/u/3Jq06E

2. https://books2read.com/u/3Jq06E

About the Author

Kay Duncan is a trailblazing five-star romance novelist, celebrated as the first romance author to be published in eBook format and a perennial bestseller for her renowned romance publisher. With a prolific career spanning multiple genres, she has captivated readers with her enchanting romance novels and visionary sci-fi fantasy romances—often dubbed "romantasy." Remarkably, one of her sci-fi fantasy works foreshadowed the internet before its widespread existence, showcasing her extraordinary imagination and foresight.

Beyond fiction, Kay's insightful writing has graced the pages of prestigious publications like the *St. Petersburg Times*, *Tampa Tribune*, and *Philadelphia Inquirer* as a contributing correspondent. She has also ventured into non-fiction, offering her expertise and compelling narratives to a broader literary audience.

A true pioneer and gifted storyteller, Kay Duncan continues to leave an indelible mark on the literary world, blending passion, innovation, and boundless creativity in every work she crafts.

www.ingramcontent.com/pod-product-compliance
Lightning Source LLC
LaVergne TN
LVHW090421210926
848480LV00002B/640
* 9 7 9 8 2 3 1 9 5 5 9 5 4 *